Am I a Terrorist?

A Cluster of Poems

notionpress
.com

Am I a Terrorist?

A Cluster of Poems

MUSKAN CHANANA

notionpress.com

Notion Press

Old No. 38, New No. 6

McNichols Road, Chetpet

Chennai - 600 031

First Published by Notion Press 2015

ISBN 978-93-5206-459-5

Poems of War and Peace

My poetry book is dedicated to my maternal grandfather, Shri KL Mahajan, who left for his heavenly abode on 5 December 2014. He was a great admirer of my poetry and enjoyed reading my poems with zeal and enthusiasm. No matter how far he has gone, he will always remain with us in our hearts.

Contents

CONTENTS

Acknowledgments

My grandmother, Mrs Sunanda Mahajan, is a very affectionate lady who has always showered unbridled blessings on me.

I am a big fan of my mother, Dr Ajayita Chanana, who has always stood by me as a mentor, aiding me to face the upheavals of life. Whenever I am in despair, she extricates me from despondency, and holds my hand to take me up the rungs of the ladder of success. I owe every moment of my success to my mother. She is a drop-dead gorgeous lady, both physically and intellectually.

My father, Dr Rajeev Chanana, has been my perfect teacher and guide. Like a whoosh of the wind, he is there in a jiffy wherever his presence is required.

My younger brother, Shaurya Chanana, and my god sister, Manju

Revered Director, Principal and Teachers of St Joseph's Sr Secondary School, Chandigarh.

Mr Rupinder Singh Grewal – Director Principal

Ms Monica Chawla – Principal

My English Teachers:

Ms Pam

Ms Vandana Sebastian

Ms Lily Sebastian

Ms Priya Sebastian

My Basketball Coach:

Ms. Paramjit Kaur Sandhu

Am I A Terrorist?

I was born as a child prodigy with profuse talent. I was indoctrinated and trained to be a terrorist. My talent was nurtured by my parents and my school in a way that would cause devastation, total chaos and the killing of innocent people in the name of God. The allurement of doing such acts lay in that I would go directly to heaven.

I am wearing a vest loaded with explosives. I am moving at a pace in a crowded place; I can hear my heart beat; I am ready to press the button and look what would have happened!

It was 30th August; the Commonwealth Games had ended.

The beauty of Glasgow, the arrangements made for the participants were splendid.

Everything was so meticulous; so well prepared,

On every TV channel, my name was being aired.

The need of each participant was given care,

The hospitality was fabulous and seemed rare.

To Hampden Park, I was so excited to go,

A golden opportunity for my abilities to be shown;

If I hadn't been here, many people in the air I would have blown!

AM I A TERRORIST?

You might be thinking who I am;
Is it the truth or am I telling you a lie?
Well, I was that person about to take many lives,
Killing people, including children and wives.
I was five when I underwent rigorous training,
As every part of my body pained, I was sternly told, "No complaining!"
Doctored videos, my elders, parents and teachers would show me,
Including how the 19 men in 9/11 reached heaven in glee.
On me, all these videos and teachings had a grave impact,
With no education, I got entangled in their web; that's a fact.
Finally the dreaded day came,
When I was supposed to play the deadly game,
I was sixteen at that time,
About to give way to, what I realize now, was a heinous crime,
It was true in practicality and not a mime.
I reached the market square,
In this match, I was the key player.
To blow away hundreds of people, I was perfectly prepared,
In my bag, explosives, pistols and detonators were perfectly layered.
I had no tension, anxiety or fear,
To me, my teachings, heaven and God were dear.
Then, in a flash of light, two people held my hands tightly,
I tried to wriggle out, but couldn't move my hands even slightly.
Despite my desperate struggling, I was caught,

"I am going away from my God," was my only enraged thought.

I was taken to a detention centre,

A completely new world I was forced to enter,

I had never seen such a world.

My old memories soon got blurred.

I was angry for a number of days,

But it slowly started getting effaced.

All changed within me with the counseling and activities there,

I could feel the love, compassion and dedicated care.

People there were sometimes gentle, sometimes rough,

I felt more comfortable here than in my previous life, which was tough.

Since there were many games, my interest in athletics rose,

With the depletion of my anger, I gained many friends, not foes.

Everyone was ecstatic; in constructive work, my energy was being put,

As I improved as a runner, somebody came to take the size of my foot.

Guess what I got? I received brand new Nike sports shoes.

They were the perfect size- not too tight and not too loose.

Those people, impressed with me, started my coaching,

I could not swallow what around me was happening.

My stamina was appreciated by my coach,

Optimism and pinpoint focus was my approach.

I started becoming better,

I started becoming faster.

Soon I became the best in the city,

In my eyes, lay the desire of success and felicity.
Competitions after competitions, I kept on winning,
On the path of success, I was soon walking and performing.
Ecstatic, I would participate in the Commonwealth games,
So that to my nation, I could bring name and fame.
I was filled with the zeal and energy to go,
Thus, finally, I was taken to Glasgow.
I ran and ran, and I won the race,
Everyone appreciated my pace and grace.
In my memory, those golden moments are still vivid,
Many fatal charges on me could have been levied.
When I was being given the medal, I literally cried,
I reckon for the first time, my country I had glorified.
The talent, thus, nurtured positively,
Would bring laurels to oneself, family and country.

Do I want war?

The soldiers had an attitude which was feisty,
There was a curfew in every city.
In a fierce war, some kingdoms had indulged,
Not even one of them was ready to retreat and budge.
The soldiers had to fight and spy,
Many of them got injured and died.
They went into a never-ending and deep sleep,
Many bodies lay on the ground, forming a heap.
They were fighting battles, leaving many a casualty,
Ultimately, a kingdom won and celebrated its victory.
But the other's fate was shocking and demoralizing,
They never thought their kingdom would fall, instead of rising.
When the soldiers' families heard about their demise,
In listless despair, they refused water and rice.
They never thought so soon they would bury their sons,
They thought after victory, they and their sons would have fun.

To add to this, an epidemic broke out,
It affected the countrymen, whether skinny or stout.
Thus, farmers were unable to produce grains,
The kingdom faced a famine due to no rains.
The king was in a contemplative and pensive mood,
He couldn't understand, and he started to brood.
People were constantly dying,
Their distraught families were crying.
"What led to the death of the loved ones?"
It was actually the end result of those hated guns.
On one side, there was ecstasy,
And on the other side, despondency.
Was this win really worth the win,
In which there was a pool of blood in the dustbin?
Had both the sides lived in peace,
Had they lived at eternal ease,
There wouldn't have been a single sinner,
Not a single family would have lost its bread winner.
Further Obama has proved it vehemently right,
Osama and his dreadful deeds are out of sight,
In such wars, many innocent lives are lost,
A bleak future ahead, and nothing of which to boast.
Find a peaceful way to end this tribulation,
Surely, if we think deeply, not far is the solution.
I WANT PEACE! I WANT PEACE! I WANT PEACE!

A Wrong Silence

Silence has become an inseparable part of a common man's life,
For one, it is vital to be quiet, but as sharp as a knife.
Nowadays, if you have witnessed a major crime,
You have to think whether your family or society is prime.
As your name will be on the top of that killer's list,
Either you will be killed or injured by his gang's fists.
So that's why, by your family, you are advised to keep quiet,
Because they can't bear to see you being a part of a killer riot.
"Keep silent! Keep silent!" You are always told,
Your family gets frightened when you try to be bold.
And be the part of the disease called 'THE KILLING IN THE COLD.'
To fight this menace of crime, be strong and brave,
To send the criminals of heinous crimes to their just grave.

Education

Something, on which you can blindly trust,
It's education and for everyone it's must.
You can trust as it is your true mate,
Very soon it will change your fate.
Wonderful it looks like a bait,
Catch it before it is too late.
It makes you walk with your head high,
Confidence is high up in the sky.
Education stands as a pedestal of innovation,
With open arms, it always offers us an invitation.
Walk on the path of success, be a winner,
Without it, one is bound to be a sinner.

Where did I go wrong?

I was determined, with my will power strong,
I failed; I don't know where I went wrong.
Whether I won or lost, still I would try,
No failure could make me shy.
Maybe the path was a bit treacherous,
Maybe my execution was a bit reckless.
Maybe the competition was tough,
Maybe the path was slippery and rough.
No matter what it was,
I would never take a pause.
My target was in sight,
I needed to get my act right,
Vehemently, and with might,
With gusto, I would fight,
To make my future bright.
Determined with my will power strong,
No one would ever say, somewhere I went wrong.

Life is a joyful journey

Life starts when you take birth,
Life starts when you step on the pious earth.
Life starts when you rise from a deep nap,
Life starts when you have fun on your mother's lap.
Life then takes a sharp turn when you learn to walk,
Now you are able to open problems, and all their locks.
You are full of joy because you can move around freely,
You don't have to be guarded by your mother's eyes surely.
Schooling is the next vital stage,
Some are happy while going, others drenched in rage.
There you are ecstatic; studying, learning and playing,
But for some, it's a nightmare as they commit suicide on failing.
Oh, our joyful journey so far comes to a halt,
Because in our studies there had been some fault.
But NO, we don't realize it when we are taking our lives,
We forget our joyous moments with parents, in our cozy bee hive.

We think it is like a film where, "What we think, is what we get,"
But sometimes, our future is different from our present, I bet.
Learn from those students at the pinnacle of success,
They excel in every country, whether India or Texas.
In a nutshell, you will face ups and downs,
Depends on you, if you accept it with smiles or frowns.
My dear friend! Life is a picturesque scenery; glow with pride,
Be strong and bold enough to take everything in your stride.
Again making a joyful journey, let's move on,
Be happy and diligent, be not a moron.
Time comes when we start becoming old,
We remain seated on chairs of oak,
But do remember old is gold.
Then slowly, memories begin to unfold.
Life ends with joyous moments in our bag,
Life ends when we go into a deep nap.
Life ends when all our secrets, truths and joys are buried in the sand,
Life finally ends when we, with our relatives, break all bands.
So actually, life is a journey which has a start and an end,
In life, joyous and bad moments perfectly blend.
But as I have learnt…

MUSKAN CHANANA

Life is happiness,
Life is forgiveness,
Life is experience,
Life is an aromatic essence,
Life is being lively in every sense,
So finally,
Life is a joy of untold proportion,
Let us enjoy it with ecstasy and elation.

God, Where Are You?

God! There is an urgent need to create a new world,
As an excess of abusive language, missiles and bombs have been hurled.
People have become so violent,
They have lost their skill of being calm and silent.
Now they talk half-heartedly to others,
Whereas, in the past, they considered everybody their brothers.
Each sees the other with a feeling of jealousy,
To say all are humane is just a fallacy,
They can't tolerate anybody's good fate,
Forget about thinking of others as their mates.
Now God, you have to come down,
And at these people, you have to frown.
Or they'll ruin everything on the earth, village and town.
Yes, God, very well you have created this clown,
To mend his ways, please, urgently come down.

Cricket

Cricket is our indomitable passion,
These days, hockey is not in fashion.
Although it's our national game,
We are trying to forget its name.
Game fixing in cricket is at its peak,
Bookies won't let any information leak.
A surfeit of people in this mess are involved,
Famous personalities too, I have been told.
Matches are fixed, we all know,
Still to buy tickets, we stand in a row.
We criticize everyone for a match fixing crime,
But we overlook everything after some time.
Look, our favorite cricketer hits sixes beyond the stadium road,
Forget it; come on; none of us are getting bored.
We are proud of our wonderful nation,
No doubt, cricket is our indomitable passion.

Help in adversity; show some generosity!

The earthquake victims are calling you,
The flu victims are following you.
The catastrophe has taken many lives,
Desperate children, men and their wives.
Shaken are their hopes and vibes,
Nature hell-bent on just hurling jibes.
There is only a scintilla of hope,
Extricate them from this grope.
It's time to be wiser,
I know you aren't a miser.
Donate generously, as much as you can,
On human kindness there is no ban.
You are the epitome of generosity,
Be the first to help in this adversity.

Friends

Friends are good and awesome,
They make our relationship blossom.
You can count on a true friend, for sure,
As a true friend's heart is always pure.
But some friends are in disguise,
So keep a check before they mesmerize.
They look smart and wise,
Keep yourself away from all their lies;
Their heart is filled with jealousy,
That's their only true legacy.
But a true friend is like a diamond,
For you, he can run any errand.
In fact, a true friend is so sweet,
Such a friend is sometimes hard to meet.
In need, a true friend is like a mother,
Stands shoulder to shoulder like a brother.
In adversity, a true friend takes the lead,
It's rightly said, "A friend in need is a friend indeed."

Jai Hind

We are all proud to be Indian,
We are one; we say it with elation.
Caste, creed, religion cannot divide us,
Love, sincerity and unity will only guide us.
Our military has won many wars,
They are our only superstars.
Many brave soldiers have lost their lives,
Leaving behind innocent children and weeping wives.
Tell the enemies we are ready to take them head-on,
To lead with example, we Indians are born.
Our belief can never be molded or shattered,
Our religion is brotherhood which can't be battered.
We promise to keep the tricolor fluttering high,
No one will live in poverty; our economy will touch the sky.
Slow and steady, we will surely win this race,
Stand up and chant JAI HIND with passion and grace…

Merry Christmas

To Bethlehem, they were going,
Nazareth, they were leaving.
'They' were Joseph and Mary, everyone knows them well,
The good news had been given to them by Gabriel, the angel,
Mother Mary would give birth to the son of God,
His name would be Jesus; he would be a great Lord.
But when they reached Bethlehem, they were shocked,
The inns were full and the houses were locked.
Maybe for that little child, God had destined something else,
Maybe the Almighty didn't want him born in rich ambience, with ringing bells.
Maybe the Lord wanted to give him the simplest environment he could,
And consequently, Jesus was born in a manger made of cheap wood.
In one shed, animals, hay and Jesus were all together,

Whereas such a godly child deserved a crib of silk and feather,
Mother Mary gave birth to Jesus in an environment like this,
Jesus was laid on the manger, receiving mother Mary's kiss.
Out spread Jesus' positive and charming aura,
It reached the outskirts of Bethlehem, full of flora,
Everyone visited the stable to see their next burgeoning king.
They brought gifts and many beautiful rings,
Wise men and women also turned up.
They brought myrrh and gold cups,
This indicated the emergence of a new world.
Where everyone was as free as a bird,
Heralding a change towards a society where the righteous could do anything,
Not, in any case, would he be whipped or beaten by a king.
Felicity, ecstasy and prosperity would be all around,
Bright blue the sky, green the nature, and lush green the ground.
No terror, no fear, no bloodshed and no rage,
This is what Jesus had envisaged.
So let's vow on these twelve days of Christmas,
We will feed ourselves with the kind words of Jesus.
Let us not go against the wishes of everyone,
Try to understand each other, and stand united as one.
Don't kill or paralyze anybody; don't make anybody blind,
Treat everyone as if she or he was your own child.

So dear readers, I hope you understand this,
Spread happiness and always live in bliss.
To end, recall the affection behind this auspicious Christmas Day,
Let's all come together merrily and just say -
Merry Christmas Merry Christmas Merry Christmas

It's high time

Farmers are weak and in a loan net,
How can they repay their huge debt?
Remember they have given us much to eat,
Is this the way to repay their lovely treat?
It's high time the government waived their loan,
Long ago, this generosity should have been shown.
Bribery is rampant in every nook and cranny,
Not only a few, corrupt people are many,
Bribery is a sin, why don't you understand?
You will land up in jail; strong is the law of the land.
It's high time the government took strict action,
It is the only way to make India a strong nation.
Whistle blowers are burnt alive for no fault of theirs,
Why? They exposed corruption which lies in layers.
Against innocent people, goons show their might,
The naive are bullied and horrible is their plight.
It's high time the police took strict action,
I am sure one day we will become an ideal nation.

Humanity

Money has taken precedence over humanity,
One day it used to be the jewel of sanctity.
People are simply running haywire,
It hardly matters if one is a liar.
He is handsome, smart and funny,
Oh, dear, he has a lot of money.
Love, affection, care are mere words,
Which have flown away like migratory birds.
A child is crying, the mother is busy on Facebook,
She'll give the child junk food as she forgot to cook.
The father is busy chatting with friends,
As if he has a responsibility to change the trends.
I don't know where this world is going,
Seeds of hatred, on our own, we are sowing.
There is no one to chat with the old and aged,
All their life they walked on a path so rugged.
Let us vow to give value to relations and emotions,
To lead our life with ecstasy and full of elation.

Give me your hand

'Give me your hand' depicts the plight of a girl stuck in a civil war. This song is dedicated to those people who are in despair and melancholy due to such wars.

This world is so bad, Just don't be like that,
This is really very sad.
Just give me your hand.
I want to come out of this darkness,
I want to be in heaven.
I want to rise and rise and rise,
I don't want to be the one who fails and cries.
This world is so bad,
Just don't be like that,
This is really very sad.
Just give me your hand
There is so much terror here,
Many selfish skeletons are here.

There is bloodshed all around
Red has stained the ground
So just give me your hand
I want to step on the land,

AM I A TERRORIST?

I just don't want to be in this ditch,
But in the great heaven,
God, that's when
I call for your help
To come and save me
From this dreadful world
I am just a little girl who is stuck here
And striving hard for my existence
So come and drop your showers of love
And give me your hand and take me to heaven.

Freedom

"Learn, learn and just learn,
In life, it will help you to earn."
Since I was born, I have heard these words,
Oh God! I wish I was free like the birds;
They don't have to study, they don't have school,
Unlike humans, they are happy; no one makes them a fool.
They don't have periods, they don't have recess,
Unlike us, their life is not a mess.
Their life is full of joy as they are never reprimanded,
Other than freedom, nothing ever they have demanded.
Look at the birds; how high they fly,
We are happy, Oh no! That's a lie.
We are advised to do rote learning,
That's the only way to secure our earning.
They are advised to love picturesque nature,
Their life is fun and they enjoy the same stature.
Neither are there terrorists nor is there any goon,
Their life in itself is one big boon.
The birds are free and always playing,

To them there is no one who is saying.
"Learn, learn and just learn,
In life, it will help you to earn."

Nothing is impossible in life

When you were a child, you were fed with a spoon,
With determination, you contemplated being on the moon,
Hurdles, day after day, can certainly slow your pace,
But you have the power to move ahead with grace,
Despair, fear, defeat are mere words,
Crown yourself with rich victorious words,
Triumph, jubilation and success are assets well known.
Optimism with hard work is what you have always shown.
Don't lose this battle; you are here to win,
Keeping your head down is truly a sin,
Stand up before it is too late,
Hard work will open fortune's gate,
Laziness has to be assassinated with a sharp knife,
Vehemently you should say, "NOTHING IS INPOSSIBLE IN LIFE."

Magical powers

Magical powers are in everybody,
From your parents to your buddy.
You just have to explore it,
As it's a wonderful inborn gift.
Find your points which are strong,
Never do anything which is wrong.
Every opportunity should be explicitly explored,
To get a future which is shaped and carved,
You'll be a superhuman for sure,
With a heart which is so pure.
Always follow the path of sincerity,
Keep your heart filled with purity,
Everything is possible when the thoughts are good,
One can carve anything even from placid wood.
On you, God's blessings, undoubtedly, will be showered,
Blend hard work with piety, and observe the magical power.

Time

To utilize time judiciously is pertinent,
To adorn one's skills, it is important.
For one and all, time is precious,
Used prudently, it gives results efficacious.
Time flows down,
Consequences slow down.
Always think time is invaluable and precious,
In my perspective, its use should be judicious,
One needs to be prudent, wise and smart,
If utilized wisely, fruitful results these impart.
To do good, there is always paucity of time,
To waste time is more than a crime.
So remember always to use time in a wise manner,
Mark it and put it up on a well decorated banner.

Love and hatred

Love has drastically declined,
In every heart, hatred is twined.
When no religion preaches hatred,
Where did we all learn this trend?
As the percentage of love has become less,
If you find it naturally, you're really blessed.
God created man with love in his heart,
Now man and love live miles apart.
Earlier, people would say "Kudos, to you!" for your good work,
Now if you do well, danger around you will lurk.
Because most of the people can't see someone prospering,
They put hurdles all around as they can't see anyone flourishing,
Love has decreased,
Hatred has increased.
If we all want to live in peace,
Love, smile and just say cheese!

Are We Too Risk Conscious These Days?

Risk! Risk! Risk!
People literally faint after listening to this.
Their gallantry, agility and briskness have faded with time,
Their heart misses a beat when they hear about any crime.
Instead of being bold and strong,
They don't get out of the house, which, I think, is wrong.
I know that rape, robbery and murder are at their peak,
But it doesn't mean that you stay at home with furniture made of teak.
You have to take risks and move out,
Lest you turn into a person who is timid and stout.
God has created you to have fun in this adventurous life,
To be bold and strong, you should always strive.
I am sorry to say that animals are better than humans,
As they run and are not afraid of shooters' guns.
Around you, learn from everything,
And to take risks, you have to give it a think.
Be brave and don't be afraid,
And you can give yourself an A^+ grade.

Boko Haram abducts girls

With love showers from God we have been graced,
We are fortunate to be born on his earth, in peace and solace,
The perfect paradigm of beauty and serenity is nature,
These qualities in our mind and soul can be nurtured,
But we have a devil and angel residing within us,
Whomsoever we feed starts growing inside us,
But these days, the demons have gone beyond their boundaries,
So self centered, they don't listen to anybody's cries and pleas,
Girls in their teens had been abducted,
Not just two or three, but about two hundred,
They were in the examination hall writing a test,
Striving hard to live and to do their best.
Unaware of what they had in their casket of fate,
Unheeding that it was their last time with friends and mates,
To be educated was their fault,
To be in school was their fault,
To have high ambition was their fault,

AM I A TERRORIST?

According to Boko Haram, being a girl was their fault,
In science, humans have reached very far,
In technology, they have crossed all bars,
On the contrary, orthodox ideas do prevail
Still in many areas, we look up to males,
These girls had been parted from their mothers
Far away from their sisters and brothers,
While we are in the most comfortable zone we have ever seen,
These girls face the hardest times of their life that can ever be,
Atrocities, tortures and murders are rampant,
One day, Boko Haram will have to pay and they will repent,
Till that time we should continue our fight against this evil fox,
Trust me, it is not as cumbersome as penetrating Fort Knox.
We just have to remain strong in the toughest times,
Even though we become the victims of moral crimes,
Yes, we will fight it out!
Yes, we will fight it out!
Should be our motto,
Just step into the fight
Like Miss Malala, without much ado.

A love tale of Cleo and Alison

A man was on the beach,
Wearing an overall of the color peach.
His overall was ragged and worn out,
He was not financially sound, but stout.
He had no gizmos and gadgets,
His hands used to fidget.
He had a wrinkled face,
He had a turtle's pace.
He had grizzled hair,
To meet the town's mayor, qualifications he had none,
No money, no luxuries; he could merely buy a bun.
Actually his wife was the earning person,
Beautiful she was; her name was Alison.
Presently this man, Cleo, was anxious and desperate,
Alison was on a cruise; her ship already two days late.
In anxiety, he moved up and down,
Because of his appearance, he could be dubbed a clown.
He couldn't sleep for the following days,
Every morning he went to the beach to gaze.

AM I A TERRORIST?

Desperately, he used to look for his wife,
And wonder if she was dead or alive.
On the ship, his wife would cook; mop the floor along with other members,
She would also sweep and brush the oil chambers.
Many days passed; no clues, no news,
He would sit on an armchair and muse.
Opposite the windows, he kept sitting there,
Overlooking the sea's shine and flare.
Like wild fire, some awful news spread,
A piece of news like a volcano erupted;
It appeared that pirates were demanding huge sacks of gold,
That was the ransom to save all who were on board.
There was none to take care,
The only option was to go to the mayor.
Cleo's dream was to meet the mayor,
But he never knew how his dream would get its flare.
Rumors slowly spread,
Abductees were being tortured.
On the shore, two bodies reached,
Identified as abductees; everyone got scared.
The mayor ordered for the bodies' burial,
The ceremony was given due importance as it was crucial.
Finally, the day of exchange arrived,
People were nervous and engaged.
The ransom was released,

The tension was eased.
Both the parties went their own way,
They were quite happy and gay.
Cleo and Alison were thrilled to meet after such a long time,
This period had been like that of a murderer facing a crime.
At home, Cleo dressed Alison's cuts and bruises,
With Cleo's love, she forgot the torture on the cruise.
Cleo felt that he had been granted a lease of life,
He was more than ecstatic to be with his wife,
Then the two bodies flashed in his mind,
He thought to himself God was truly kind.
He thought, "Why do people indulge in heinous acts?
Why do they behave like unbridled brats?
Why is everyone running after money?
Is it the world's only pot of honey?
Such money will not give anyone joy,
To go to hell, it's one's own ploy.
Introspect and refrain from such acts,
Mend your way before the Almighty reacts.
He gives justice to one and all,
For him, even an ant is not small.
Let's make the world a peaceful place,
Respect each other and live with grace."

Mother Nature

Nature is an asset which we should all relish. At the same time, it should be respected and taken care by one and all. The more you respect it, the more it will take care of your well-being. Hurricanes, floods, earthquakes and other natural calamities can be attributed to human greed to a certain extent. I have composed a few poems highlighting the grief of Mother Nature. Don't whip your mother, love her! These poems mark our respect for Mother Nature...

A letter from the wind

Trees sway when I blow,
Plants rejoice when I flow.
When plants get energized and stimulated,
Nature turns serene and is never infuriated.
I am the moving air,
I am this earth's au pair.
I blow around with a gentle breeze,
Whispering and making your life one of ease.
Everything had gone well for millions of years,
Then I realized something dire, from which I developed fear.
A large monstrous figure is engulfing our earth,
It is spreading sorrow and not any kind of mirth.
This monster is developing at a very fast rate,
I don't know what would be mine and my fellows' fate.
This monster has taken birth due to human greed,
Pollution, Air conditioners, vehicles, factories take the lead.
Gl- ob- al W-ar-ming, it is without an iota of doubt,
I consider humans are, undoubtedly, louts.

Gl- ob- al W-ar-ming has such a negative fame,
That without stammering, I can't say its name.
Now when I blow, I don't notice any greenery,
Now when I blow, I don't see any picturesque scenery.
I mostly see drought, famine, floods and fallow lands,
I do see industries where once there used to be grassland.
I see the animal kingdom in dismay and despair,
Oh! Is there anybody to give them love and care?
When they lose their habitat, they move to cities and towns,
Even the lion king is killed and has to part with his crown.
Don't kill and torture them by taking their homeland,
Don't convert the forest patches into a wasteland.
I see the same anguish in the eyes of polar animals,
Humans are not less than ruthless cannibals.
For the Frigid Zone animals, I truly feel sad,
Because ice has started melting, which is really bad!
I also have a tough time seeing disaster before my eyes,
Humans do nothing for the environment; they just tell lies.
There are so many poisonous gases around me,
I can see them acting as my coffin keys.
I am also getting so suffocated here,
I know my death is, indeed, quite near.
I have realized that nature will vanish soon,
For dear humans, it's a bane and not a boon.
One day, you will gasp for air and long for life,
Wake up, humans, the time has come to strive.

Do something sensible or in hell you will be pinned,
This letter is from-
Yours sincerely,
The Wind.

Deforestation

One girl, Serica, was walking by the shore,
Generosity was filled in her heart's core.
I am talking about a quiet serene night,
The moon gleams rendered a picturesque sight.
Her dog came running to her,
She began to ruffle its fur.
There was peace surrounding them,
The scene was worth a million dollar gem.
Suddenly came the sound of the cutting down of trees,
Serica followed the sound, and what did she see?
The people cutting trees were none other than her family friends,
She stopped in shock and said, "Oh no! The world ends."
Everybody suddenly halted,
Their faces, flabbergasted.
They asked, "Serica, why are you stopping us?"
Her mother told her, "Go home and don't make a fuss."
She tried to stop and impede their activity,
The feeling that rose in her mind was that of pity.

When the activity was finally turned down,
She glared at them with a frown.
Serica said, "Now, for God's sake, look around."
Everyone's tongue in their mouth was as if bound,
Lush green ground had turned into a brown one,
They all felt sorry, but the damage had already been done.
Serica said, "Do you realize now what a big mistake you have made?"
As in front of them, a surfeit of trees was laid.
They themselves had to bear the blame,
Heads down, they all stood in shame.
Serica explained to them the importance of afforestation,
They agreed with her in a moment of elation.
She explained how it was no one's gain,
They vowed never to do it again.
So the girl though, being small,
Stopped those, who were strong and tall.
From then, the girl was always helped by the guys,
To spread the message; by cutting trees, you can say to Nature 'Goodbye!'

Beautiful Nature

Nature! Where have you gone?
Haven't seen you since I was born.
Now this question will always arise,
Once you were a very precious prize.
Once you were full of greenery,
Where is that splendid scenery?
You give us whatever we need,
Still on the top is our greed.
You give us oxygen, you keep us fit,
You give us food in plenty, not just a bit.
Undoubtedly, it is a precious gift,
Let's strive hard to keep it fit.
We children vow to plant a tree,
The only way we can fill you with glee.

Wrath of Nature

Wrath! Wrath! It erupts suddenly,
Nature can also do it knowingly.
The bad deeds of humans have filled her bowl,
That's why loathing for humans has taken its toll.
She can do this any time,
Tampering with nature is a crime.
Cut down trees and she will glare,
Floods and landslides will be there.
And humans will run like small hares,
A feeling of panic will be filled in the air.
In its anger, no one will be spared,
Friends! Like a baby, it needs to be cared.
Before it's too late, understand and take care,
For us it's a lifeline; save it; it's my humble prayer.

Nature

Nature goddess, are you angry with us?
For the pollution emanating from our buses and trucks?
I am sorry on behalf of other people,
Because of us, your whole nature family has become feeble.
I can understand how sad you feel,
But I am trying my best to make you heal.
By telling people of your importance and usage,
They listen to me just as they heed a wise sage.
But they are not bringing a change in themselves,
They destroy you, feeling you'll recover through the magic of elves.
I will make them understand your importance,
Tell them to create between pollution and nature a fence.
I will surely try my level best,
So that you are respected as a loved guest.

Save Me

It was a bright sight,
One boy was flying a kite.
Nature was all around,
Green was the ground,
Birds were making chirping sounds,
The kite was flying round and round.
It was such a beautiful tale to tell,
It was not something at which you could yell.
It was much finer than a piece of art.
On one flowing stream, there was a raft,
Two people were sitting on it,
In the river, throwing in some garbage bits.
My heart broke,
My throat choked,
I wondered how they could do so,
Without any sweat of regret on their brow.
If we spoil our Mother Earth,
Then who will give us nature and birth.
Please try to understand,

We have a natural gift which is grand.
If we don't care about it, we will have to be sad.
So do take much care
Of the biggest animal to the smallest hare.
And let's keep this nature very pious,
So that the ways to destroy it are scarce.

Save Mother Earth

My lovely earth is being polluted.
In the past, it was respected and saluted.
It used to be loved by all,
And was everybody's best pal.
Earlier people used to respect its qualities.
But now what is seen on earth are just cruelties.
People are polluting every part of this earth
Just for their entertainment and mirth.
Why do people not understand the importance of this place?
It is a crucial and serious case.
Everyone from humans to wildfowl,
And from the smallest organism to the fish in the bowl,
Want a place like earth to live in.
So do your best,
It's your test,
It's not just a jest.

"How Enterprising!" A Voice Said As I Closed the Door Behind Me

Every company wants to be at the apex of success,
No matter whether in India or Texas.
In their dreams, they see their homes inundated with money,
They just want to excel and eat the best quality honey.
They become the inventors of many different ads,
They want more publicity for their various brands.
While watching television, such an ad was aired,
Created by a reputed company; with my parents it was shared.
The company actually wanted to manufacture new things,
They wanted to make something extraordinary, instead of those mundane rings.
They wanted to seek help from the masses,
So the people were allowed to give ideas, from all the different classes.
Every person thought of a product after seeing that ad,
I was also one of them; when an idea struck my mind, I was glad.

I thought about things made for women's protection,
I reckoned it would be useful for society's every section.
I told my idea to my parents and friends,
They approved of it; lauded it as one of the latest trends.
The next day I visited their office and explained what I thought,
They became really jubilant, having liked the idea a lot.
As I was going out, closing the door behind me,
I heard a voice whisper, "How enterprising!" as they were all having tea.
On hearing this, I rushed in haste after shutting the door,
I ran to my parents who, in the waiting room, were getting bored.
"Oh, my God," they exclaimed, when they heard about it,
They became exuberant and wanted to award me a gift.
I wanted them to choose me as the winner,
As my product would be a bane for all sinners.
However, I can never forget the words, "How enterprising!"
And I wish I could keep succeeding and rising.

I Knew This Was My Moment

Thank you, God, for giving me everything that I need,
Thank you for planting in my life, a success seed.
My success in life started when I was in the seventh class,
I turned into gold from a cheap metal like brass.
Before that, in school I used to enjoy victory,
I had never dreamt of performing in a populous territory.
I was sad, depressed and in grief,
Wondering when I could win a competition, and have some relief.
Luckily that moment wasn't too far,
And I kept on breaking every hindrance, every bar.
I became a conscientious and an industrious student,
While taking any decision, I was always prudent.
My parents told me not to lose heart,
So I excelled in the written and speaking art.
An opportunity knocked on my door,
I was exuberant and wanted to know more.
It was actually a declamation contest,
I knew this was my moment; I wanted to be the best.

I practiced for it with all my strength,
My parents used to chastise me for speaking rapidly at length.
They would say, "Speak slowly but with determination,
And you will win as, for you, there will be no elimination."
One day before, I was doing my chores in a rhythmic movement,
I was not at all nervous because I knew this was my moment.
Finally, the day came and I was told how to speak; I did the same,
I was desperate to succeed and make a name.
Guess what! I won, as I spoke meticulously, following the rules,
Many children had come; in total, there were thirty-five schools.
This moment gave me a fillip to do even more,
I rose higher and higher, and in the sky I soared.
Then in the eighth, I played three nationals of basketball,
On the road to success, I just rolled on.
In the School Tribune, my poem 'Wrong Silence' was published,
I was happy; I really thrived and flourished.
In the tenth, of twenty Indian girls, I was chosen to go to Japan,
Mom's words reverberated, "Believe in Karma; success will come in a short span".

Whether it is good or bad, one has to remain strong,
Losing heart and hope is absolutely wrong.
In the end, I say, "Thanks, God, for dropping this opportunity in my hand.
Thanks, for revealing my moment; my happiness will stretch like a rubber band.
Thank you! Thank you! Thank you! For telling me this was my moment!"
I knew in my heart; it was my very own moment.